ODE TO THY Apricot

REVISITED

DENNIS W. C. WONG

Ode To Thy Apricot: Revisited
Copyright © 2023 by Dennis W. C. Wong

All rights reserved. No part of this publication may be reproduced, distributed, or transmitted in any form or by any means, including photocopying, recording, or other electronic or mechanical methods, without the prior written permission of the publisher, except in the case brief quotations embodied in critical reviews and other noncommercial uses permitted by copyright law.

ISBN: (Paperback)   978-1737241171
        (e-book)   978-1737241188

The views expressed in this book are solely those of the author and do not necessarily reflect the views of the publisher, and the publisher hereby disclaims any responsibility for them.

Clever Clock Press

Contents

Prologue 1

The Ode and the New....................... 1

Who Am I................................. 2

The Colors of Our Marriage 4

Your Gentle Touch 5

The Twelve Years of Marriage................ 6

Joy to the World 8

It Started Out by Chance 9

ERICA 10

My Journey............................... 11

My Vow 12

There is a Young Woman from Maryland 13

Adorned Beauty 16

I Ran.................................... 18

The Golden Years 20

I Plan to Retire 21

Ancient Chinese Folklore 22

A New Episode 24

Six...................................... 25

Sheryll 26

Your Face 27

Sunset to Sunrise 28

Today 29

Tee Time 30

My Falcon Car 32

Retire Meant 34

Appy Retires 35

Send 36

To the Moon 37

ABC's 38

Will You Be My Friend? 39

A Cup of Joe 40

Cough Fee 41

I Am Not a Poet 42

Prologue

 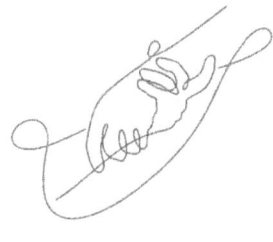

The Ode and the New

The ode and the new
brings me to the beginning of the queue.
I don't know when;
I didn't know then.
Knowledge and commitment
are goals towards achievement.
There is a proverb to teach,
and it exists within your reach.
A pen in hand
is mighty in this land.
The foundation of the words we seek
manifests beneath the words we speak.
The new and the old
are treasures to behold.

March 1, 2023

Who Am I

Who am I?
        I ask you why?
        I am just a guy
        about to die.

        The path ahead is dry
        as I traverse up very high;
        I think I got something in my eye
        or maybe it is just a stye.

        So, who I am?
        I am not Sam,
        but I do love Spam,
        and I know who I am.

All I want to be
        is me.

August 18, 2021

Poems to my wife, Jocelyn

The Colors of Our Marriage

Green represents hope and our future.
    Red is for the love we share.
    I am the yellow rose.
    You are my black beauty,
    and together, we form a unity.

Dennis W.C. Wong
February 9, 1994

Your Gentle Touch

I don't ask for much,
> just your gentle touch.

I miss
your kiss,
a smile on your face,
and your arms to embrace.
You are my number one
under the sun,
and whenever I hear your voice,
I know I made the right choice.

> *Your loving husband*
> *Always and forever,*
> *Dennis*
> *February 8, 1997*

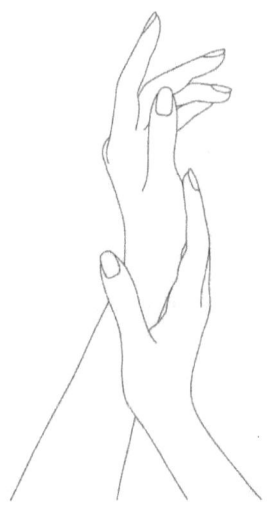

The Twelve Years of Marriage

On the first year of marriage, my true love gave to me
a Buddha in a bonsai tree.

On the second year of marriage, my true love gave to me two
turtle DSE's.
On the third year of marriage, my true love gave to me
three Cornish hens.

On the fourth year of marriage my true love gave to me
four origami birds.

On the fifth year of marriage, my true love gave to me
five gold earrings.

On the sixth year of marriage, my true love gave to me
six hares a-laying.

On the seventh year of marriage, my true love gave to me
seven fishes swimming.

On the eighth year of marriage, my true love gave to me
eight maids a-crying.

On the ninth year of marriage, my true love gave to me
nine children dancing.

On the tenth year of marriage, my true love gave to me
ten frogs a-leaping.

On the eleventh year of marriage, my true love gave to me
eleven stoves a-piping.

On the twelfth year of marriage, my true love gave to me
twelve drummers vowing.

I vow to you, my love,
on earth and to the heaven above
to be with you happily
for as long as you need me.

Dennis Wong
January 28, 1998

Joy to the World

Joy to the world
>	where a baby girl,
>	long ago the Carters celebrated,
>	a precious child created.

In a little town of Maryland,
>	she left footprints in the sand.
>	She grew up strong
>	in a world where we belong.

With wisdom and fire,
>	for all to admire,
>	I loved you then.
>	You are my Godsend.

Two fine young men,
>	Zarek and Kayin,
>	from our union, behold.
>	Joy to the world.
>	Amen.

Love,
Dennis
December 24, 2012

It Started Out by Chance

It started out by chance
        in unusual circumstance.
        You were there
        to style my hair.

A Cancer woman
        meets a Scorpio man.
        Two different cultures
        emerge in symbolic structures.

I took you to the park
        and a movie at dark.
        A revolving clock
        holds the key to unlock
        the memories of our first date
        that encapsulated our fate.

You came every night
        and left before daylight.
        It started out by chance
        and ended in romance.

August 17, 2021

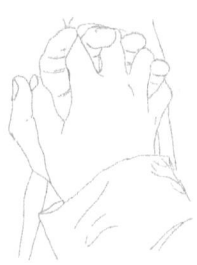

ERICA

"As You Graduate"

Go forth unto the light
and don't lose sight
of your dreams
no matter how hard it seems
at times.

As you Graduate
Go forth and
Calculate
Demonstrate
Estimate
Evaluate
Formulate
Generate
Illustrate
Initiate
Investigate
Operate
Participate
Translate
and Integrate

Into your travels throughout the land
And leave your Footprints in the Sand.

Love,
"Dad"
June 1992

My Journey

My journey is just beginning, continuing,
      with no ending.
      searching for a meaning, reasoning,
      with an understanding.

I reach out to you assisting, comforting,
      with care providing,
      and embracing each day smiling,
      with a new beginning.

Dennis W.C. Wong
April 24, 2002

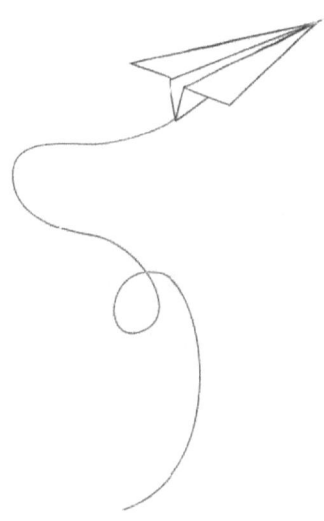

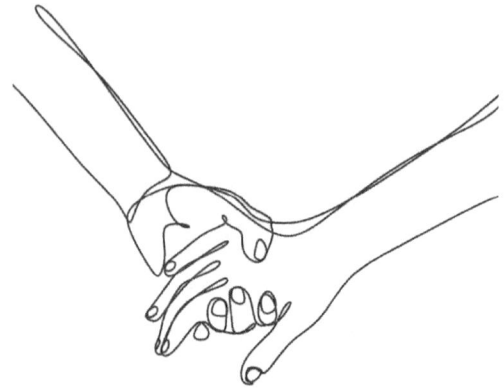

My Vow

I vow to you, my love,
    on earth and to the heaven above,
    to be with you happily
    for as long as you need me.

January 28, 1998

There is a Young Woman from Maryland

There is a young woman from Maryland,
>   who searched for her folks 'cross the land.
>   She finished a book,
>   and said, "Come and look.
>   Now, aren't their own words just grand?"

May, 2016

In Loving Memory To My Sister Debbie
October 18, 1954 - May 06, 2005

Adorned Beauty

Adorned beauty,
Natural as can be,
Precious for all to see,
In spirit, you are free.
Remembering yesterday,
Reminiscing this May.
Remembering the years,
The unknown and the fears.
Remembering all that you meant,
And the brief times that we spent.
Remembering our birthday exchanges,
Over the distant mountain ranges.
Remembering your new outlook,
And the path that you took.

A new beginning unravels;
Go placidly in your travels.
Losing you is sad,
But now you're with Dad.

Big Brother,
Dennis

I Ran

When fear encroached upon me,
    what did I do?
    I ran.

When a bear hovered over me,
    what did I do?
    I ran.

When danger approached me,
    what did I do?
    I ran.

When bullies picked on me,
    what did I do?
    I ran.

When the police surrounded me,
    what did I do?
    I ran.

When the bill collector called on me,
        what did I do?
        I ran.

When a friend gave me sugar and lemons,
        what did I do?
        I made lemonade
        under the shade,
        to quench my thirst
        at first;
        and then I ran
        as fast as I can,
        leaving footprints in the sand,
        along the rugged California coastal land.

August 29, 2021

The Golden Years

The golden years
    is not as it appears.

Looking back at all our careers,
    happiness until the time nears,
    followed by sadness and fears.

We shopped at Sears
    and ate corn by the ears.

Sought guidance from the Seers
    as we switched gears
    from champagne to beers.

August 29, 2021

I Plan to Retire

I plan to retire
      before I expire,

reminiscing my first day of hire,
      cooking chickens in pressure cookers under fire,

longing and wishing to aspire,
      acquiring a trade while I perspire,

educating at schools of learning higher,
      gathering experience to fulfill my desire,

observing caterpillars morph into stages they require,
      waiting for the butterflies as they transpire,

counting down the days to the wire,
      and reading it in the National Enquirer.

August 21, 2021

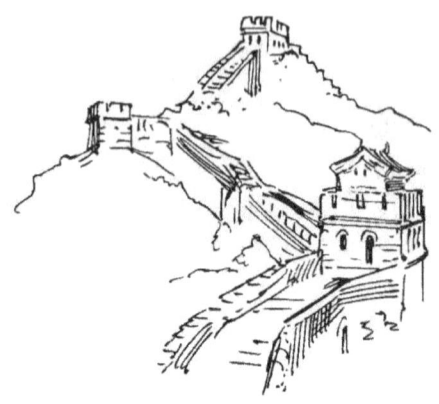

Ancient Chinese Folklore

I want to explore
> Ancient Chinese Folklore.
> I don't know what's in store
> until I leave out the door.

I was ready to soar
> from the U.S.A. to the China shore
> at half past four
> in a business suit I wore.

I want to restore
> The Ancestral Halls that I adore,
> as I tore
> into the inner core.

I started to bore,
> finding artifacts galore
> after sifting through the score,
> and admiring the decor.

There is a chore
> I would not ignore,
> using a tea kettle to pour,
> in a bowl just before.

After the encore,
> I want to do more.

April 21, 2022

A New Episode

I was told
that a new episode
is about to explode
at a theatre down the road
near an abandon abode
in the mother lode.
It could implode
during the winter cold,
and if you're bold,
you might find gold.
As I watched it unfold,
I was not truly sold.
I developed a lesion
in this artic region.
This could be a reason
to end the season.

April 19, 2022

Six

I sent you six
  so, you can start the fix,
while waiting for more,
  it's only four,
  for what's in store,
  out the door.
    It's true
      that your crew,
      with insight and a brew,
      will create the new.
    I'll see what they drew
      as they shade in the hue.

April 16, 2022

Sheryll

I signed this book unsterile
alongside Dr. Jekyll
in my scrub apparel
singing a Christmas carol
in flight with a sparrow
straight as an arrow.

Dennis W.C. Wong
01/20/2022

Your Face

To embrace
your face,
I start to trace
at my own pace
because there is no race.
To make a case
I found a place
I don't have to chase
with you poised with a vase
entwined in lace.

April 15, 2022

Sunset to Sunrise

I look forward to the sunset,
    as my ageing mind senses to forget,
    and my heart is failing as yet,
    but I embrace each day it is met.
As I go forth to say my goodbyes,
    a new dawn will rise,
    amidst the waning moon ties,
    which sheds light in front of my eyes,
    and makes my heightened emotions arise,
    from sunset to sunrise.

May 4, 2022

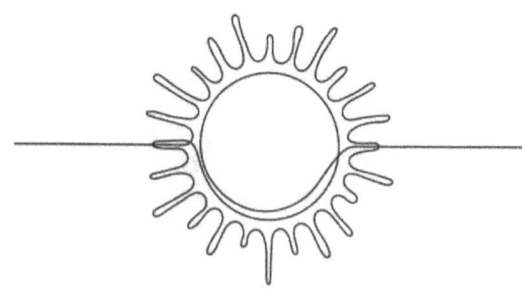

Today

What should I do today?
Find a needle in a stack of hay?
Or going on a ride in a sleigh?
If I may
Who is to say?
You said "Hey",
Let's get away
and keep things at bay.
Is that okay?
Think about it and stay.

April 15, 2022

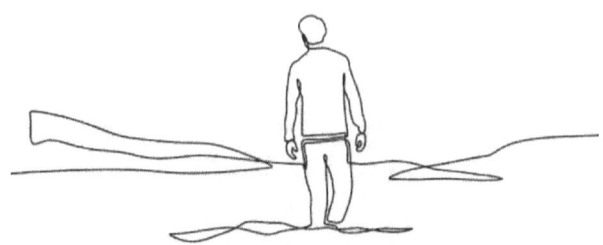

Tee Time

It's tee time.
I play for a dime.
It is not a crime,
I chime.
"Do you want to play?"
I say.
It's a gorgeous day.
Show me the way.
I rode on a cart
with Bart
from Kmart
right from the start.
At the tee,
I watched as far as I could see,
a lone cypress tree
alongside a view of the sea
with a celebrity.
After getting advice from Eddie,
my caddie,
he said when you're ready,
plant your feet and be steady.
When I swung and pivot,
I hit a divot.
As I watched my ball soar,
I let out a roar
and said "fore"
but the fans ignore.

Just wishing
but narrowly missing,
I have not seen
my ball reaching the green,
but I am on par
so far.
My back felt sore,
but I wanted more
after seeing my score,
not like before.
Let's celebrate.
I'm feeling great.
It's tea time
with lemon lime.

April 16, 2022

My Falcon Car

My Falcon car is by far a star, without a scar?
The internet salesman said "sold";
The transport truck driver drove it down the road
feeling bold
and through the cold
with no load.

A '69 Falcon Sports Coupe
soaring down with a swoop,
it took flight
dressed in Wimbledon white.

With a black-crested top
it continued non-stop
as it passed by each tower
with enough power
down a narrow strait
under a 302 V-8.

On the 2nd day
in the month of May,
the truck driver arrived.
The five-day trip, my car survived.

From Pennsylvania
to Hayward, California,
in the driveway, the Falcon he set
where my wife, he met.
And I won't forget

that I bought a rust bucket.
While I worked under the hood
in my neighborhood,
it stood
with tires blocked by wood.

I am under the gun
with restoration just begun.
I will go on a run
and have some fun
under the sun.
I'll tell you when I'm done.

Four thousand miles I had driven
in a newly rebuilt rendition,
cruising along a dusty scenery
toward Terra D' Oro Winery.

At the 10th annual Cru-Zin in the Vineyard,
the announcement was heard
that I had won
the Best Young Gun.
My Falcon continues to soar
in the American Muscle Cars Calendar 2024.

July 15,2023

Retire Meant

Retire meant
the work which I didn't resent,

sixty days I have spent,
and the places that I went,

enjoying time at my resident,
while putting up a backyard tent.

learning Psalms amidst Lent,
with prayers and forgiveness to vent.

the books that I have sent,
sales didn't make a dent,

and spending my last cent,
running for president.

April 12, 2022

Appy Retires

As Appy plans to retire,
he reminisces his first day of hire,
longing and wishing to aspire,
acquiring a trade while we all perspire,
educating at schools of learning higher,
gathering experience to fulfill his desire,
observing caterpillars morph into stages they require,
waiting for the butterflies as they transpire,
counting down the days to the wire,
and finally enjoying his fruitful endeavour.

January 23, 2022

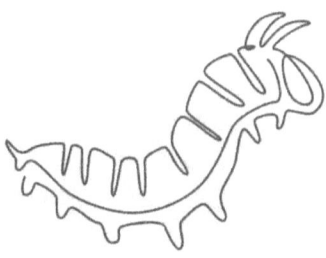

Send

To a friend,
just around the bend.

Let me recommend
that you attend
a meeting at our den.

I offer a hand to lend
to you my friend,
as I continue to mend.

In the end,
before I suspend,
I hit send.

April 17, 2022

To the Moon

I will be getting off soon
and I want to go to the moon,
planning to arrive there by noon
in the middle of June,
from my residence in Suisun
after watching a cartoon.

I felt like a kid at heart
and start
to tear things apart
from inside my cart.

I leave you my wishes
while wearing my Superman britches
which left you in stitches
and showing off my itches.

After feeding the fishes
and doing the dishes,
from a meal that was delicious,
I reach out to my Mrs.
for her parting kisses.

I'll be landing soon
near a lagoon
or on top of a ruin
and singing a tune;
I'm on the moon.

April 17, 2022

ABC's

ABC
> One two three,
> In this world including me,
> we all will be able to agree.

DEF
> We don't need a ref.

GHI
> It starts with "Hi"

JKL
> and I am doing well.

MNO
> I hope you are also,

PQR
> wherever you are,
> near and far.

STU
> just me and you,

VWX
> with callous attitudes lax.

YZ
> Let me be me.

Now I know my ABC's,
> and proud to be an American-Born Chinese.

April 10, 2022

Will You Be My Friend?

I reach out to you again and again,
seeing you at the Donut Den,
passing you a note I send,
waiting for a time to spend,
going to places to attend,
wishing for issues to amend.
I see a light in the end.
Will you be my friend?

April 14, 2022

A Cup of Joe

Where do I want to go?
To the snow?
I don't know.
The lawn needs a mow
two days in a row.
It's beginning to show
the grass is not low.
I must say "whoa"
or maybe "no".
To whomever said "so",
I say "yo"
to a cup of "Joe".

April 13, 2022

Cough Fee

When you cough,
      I spray with Off.
A cold
      can get very old
I was told
      watching things unfold.
There is a cost
      that could get lost
      during a frost
      from acrost.
Let's take
      a break
      for goodness sake
      since we are awake
      from an earthquake.
Have a cup of coffee
      on me,
      then take your meds and be
      cough free.

April 16, 2022

I Am Not a Poet

I am not a poet
and I can show it.
I started with a kit
after contemplating a bit
while I sit
in a hickory pit.
I could write a skit
and it might be a hit.
Did you catch it with a mitt?
I submit.
The poems that I knit
do not fit.
It left a divot
in a widget.
To wit:
How can I commit?
Is it legit?
I quit.

April 18, 2022

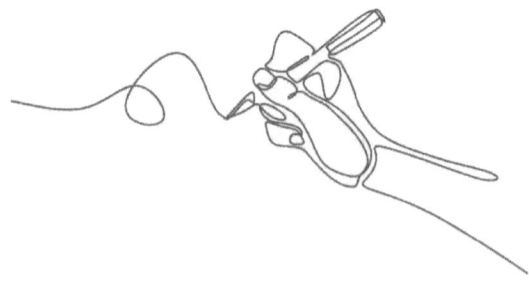

www.ingramcontent.com/pod-product-compliance
Lightning Source LLC
Chambersburg PA
CBHW070340120526
44590CB00017B/2956